Story of a Wave

a poetry book

VRUJEN

Acknowledgements

I want to express my gratitude to the creativity that flowed from my soul and the inner artist child who gave expression to its desires in ways that felt true. My heartfelt thanks go to my adult self for finally bringing this book to life after nearly five years of crafting its manuscript.

I am grateful for all those who have loved me and allowed me to reciprocate that love. Without them, the emotions and the wisdom to navigate them would not have blossomed. Each word within this book is a reflection of the loves I've encountered in my journey so far.

My appreciation extends to my parents, Rakesh and Sanjeevani, a constant presence in my life, guiding me to simplify life's complexities. Their unwavering support has nurtured my creative aspirations and enabled me to live a life full of imagination.

I wish to acknowledge my wonderful partner, Kunal, who became the haven where my soul found solace and emerged as a formidable force. He is also the illustrator for my cover page design.

Furthermore, I'd like to thank the talented Canva artists whose illustrations grace these pages. Some of the artwork is of my own creation inspired by these artists.

Last, but not least, I am indebted to my mentor, Somesh Chaddha, who has illuminated my life path and helped me find the creativity that exists in me, aiding me in discovering the rhythm within my writing and thoughts.

TABLE OF CONTENTS

Prologue

A wave in the ocean is ever growing, ever learning, ever rising and falling, meeting other waves, parting from them, crashing and calming, while the world around it keeps turning. This book has 6 chapters, Meeting, Rising, Stagnation, Crashing, Taking back and lastly, Calming Vastness, which depict the journey of a wave and also of how usually a relationship in our life goes.

Meeting is about two souls meeting, the spark, or the absence of it, the sudden shift in our being that causes us to simply flow and follow our partner into any abyss they invite us in.

Rising is about the butterflies in the stomach that flutter around when our loved ones kiss us, touch us, feel our skin, hear our breath, almost vanishing and flowing back in, with each of their breath.

Stagnation is that part of a relationship where we are clueless about whether it's going good or bad, but we are still there because it feels comfortable without any uncertainties or risks that we are avoiding to dwell on.

Crashing is that tipping point where we accept our fate and let it all go, the feelings, thoughts; hurting, crying, wailing, till we grieve what we have lost, a part of our life and the part of our own self that was in love.

Taking back the lessons learned from these experiences is something that the ocean of life does till we actually internalize and learn them. We start seeing the repeating patterns and slowly allow ourselves to break out of them.

Calming vastness is when we let ourselves flow with the currents of the big blue fields out there. Love without an expectation of something in return, love the emotion of love itself.

I hope you find some experiences, some emotions, and some words relatable, and enjoy this journey of love and life with me.

Meeting
OF TWO SOULS

IT BEGAN HERE

The flowing,
The falling,
The longing,
The trying,
           and crying,
The stalling,
The separating,
The repeating,
and repenting,
           and learning.

BECOMING

Sometimes he wonders;
Did we miss out on the flirtation,
Did we miss out on the conversation,
Did we miss out on the evaluation,
Of whether it feels right?

Yes, I say;
We did skip that part,
We did skip that brain,
We did skip that heart,
Beat,

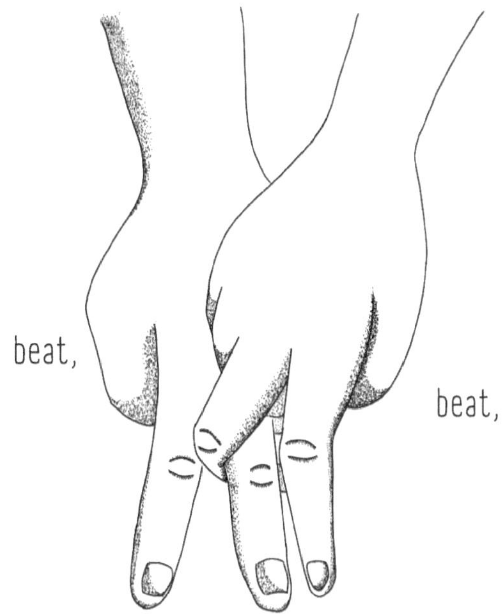

Till it got better.

I became we;
In that manner of speaking,
In that manner of listening,
In that manner of loving,
You also became we.

THEY STRIKE

The smudge of the lux,
The flow of the gush,
A thought that's naive,
It defines the dive,
The waterless tears of joy,
Of finding that favourite toy,
Sitting on some spike,
Are the notes they strike.

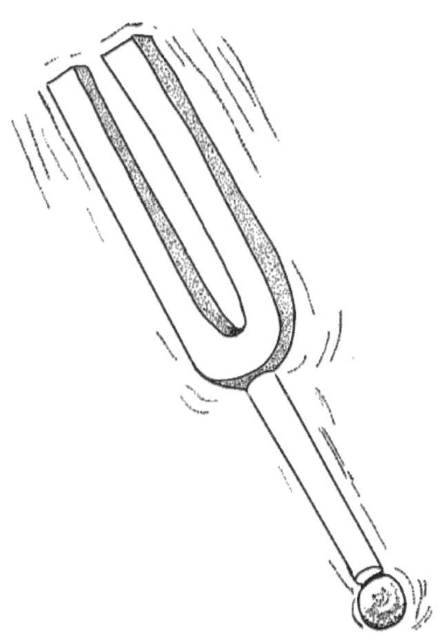

DREAMING

Thinking,
Thinking of you.

Wishing,
Wishing you could be here.

Trying,
Trying to doze off.

Dreaming,
Dreaming with my eyes open.

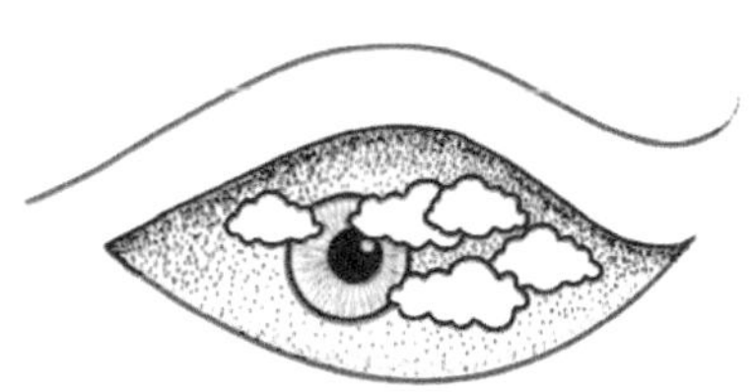

THE MOONCHILD

I don't know what Love is,
Is it just that when it's there,
One understands what it is,
Or is it just the emotion one misses,
When it isn't around.

I don't know what Love is,
Is it just the grip,
One has while treading on treacherous territories,
Or is it the treat to one's senses,
When one flies and not falls for it.

I don't know what Love is,
Is it just the flowing of the breeze,
Through the pine needles,
Or is it the aroma they infuse,
Unknowing of either's knowledge.

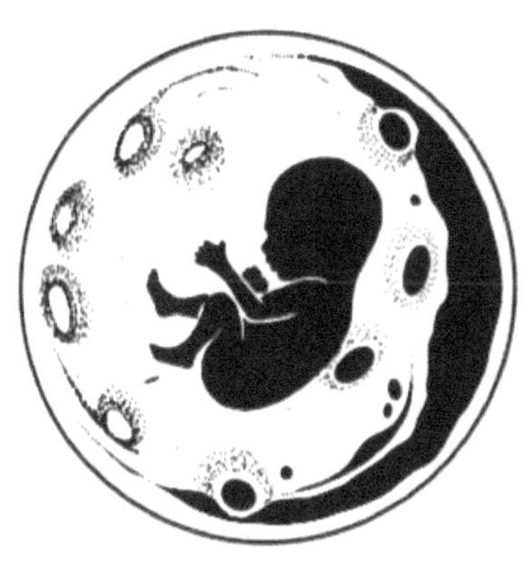

I still don't know what Love is,
Though I dive in its shallow waters,
Waxing and waning,
With the moonlight,
With the Moonchild.

I SING YOU

It's the beauty,
That captivated me,
It's you,
Who encapsulated me.

It's the technology,
That evaded me,
It's you,
Who discovered me.

It's the ballads,
That were sung to me,
It's you,
Who I sing now.

MILESTONES

Past and present he envelops,
In an elegant design,
The dream catcher he weaves,
I wonder if the feathers is where his heart is.

Ease and eccentricity he portrays,
In a dynamic painting,
The depth so real he falls,
I wonder if the fall is what he's craving for.

Smile and simplicity he infuses,
In the air around him,
On a crossing his heart stops,
I wonder if the milestones are
Just a mile apart.

MARBLE SKIN (PHASES PT. 2)

I left my mind, body and consciousness,
Transcending into someone,
Transforming into something,
I never thought I would be.

It brought back a part of me,
Long lost but flickering,
Goosebumps running all over the marble skin,
Cold, smooth, but firm and lasting.

He said, "Would it be nice?",
Conscious about my past,
I wondered, "Would it surprise me?",
Oh and it did,
Ecstasy is what I feel.

Now the skin feels incomplete,
Without the touch of the marble,
I lost my existence on a marble floor,
And found it back in a marble skin.

FLOW

Love flows from one pool to another,
I swim through,
I spin along,
I revive what's lost,
And I flow again.

Rising

OF EMOTIONS

SEDUCING

Your
lips
can't
finish
what
your
fingers
have
started.

LEVITATING

A lull,
A dull,
On the plateau,
A chateau,
Of mirrors,
Refracting,
Every sense of ours;
Left human.

A transcendental,
Coincidence,
The eclipses,
And the lapses,
Of time,
Slipping,
Out of hands;
Oft lost.

A bard,
And his love,
The emotion,
And expression,
Of the souls,
Infusing,
Into each other;
Daft them.

A knot,
Well sought,
The beauty,
And the city,
Of dreams,
Weaving,
Themselves;
L(e)V(it)ating with each other.

FINGERS

Hiding behind
nimble fingers,
Oh, pretty boy..

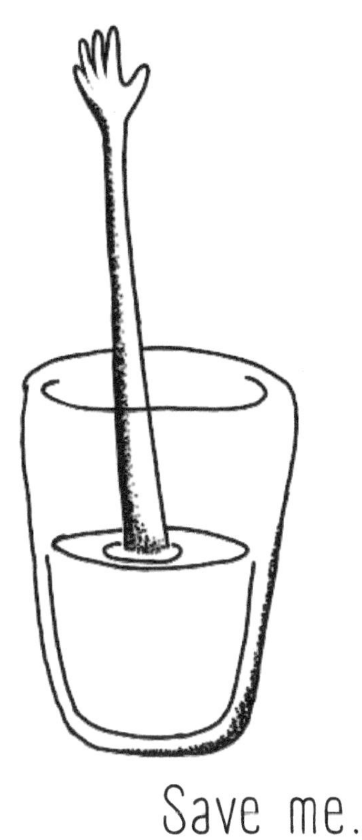

Save me.

BLURRY LINES

We tread on blurred lines,
Blurry senses guiding each,
To the other, magnetizing,
The heartbeats to the rhythm,
Of unknown, still knowing,
What it means to them.

We led our lives entangled,
In strange patterns mingling,
With stranger souls feeling,
Alone, though together,
Incomplete, though complementing,
The yin to the yang.

We paid our debts,
Of past sins, sinners we,
Forgave for their mistakes,
Forgiveness is all that is asked,
Of the hearts that broke,
On the path of finding each other.

We met the least requirements,
Of the T&C on each other's,
Thoughts about love, trusting,
This new thread woven in,
Time and space where,
Everything lies on the blurry lines.

DAZED

Suck my life through
that clogged pipe,
Blow the smoke
feeling the high,
Be dazed by the
beauty,

Till it lasts.

BLOSSOMING

The blossom that spring brings,
Is now adorned and thorned,
By the summer humm-drums.

PURSED LIPS

Pursed lips thinking of a distant future, triggers a spiral
of emotional roller coaster. The ride stops, and you want
to go again.

A calm before the thunder,
A silence before the chaos,
A pin drops and the echoes are heard for miles to the
horizon.

Lost in the shadows and silhouettes,
The periphery so intricate,
It takes you a while to soak it in.

TONGUES

We run into the wilderness,
Climbing up and down the tongues
that drummed,

We fly as light as the feather;

Swivelling down,
We sink to the ocean-floor,
Never to be found.

LIGHT

I wish to be loved,
Loved with all my flaws,
The f**ked up part of me,
And also the unf**ked part.

Objectify me,
Or make me your subject,
Of interests of different kinds,
Different worlds brought together.

Beauty lies within, you say,
So much darkness within,
Can't say be the light of my life,
But light it up for a second at least.

KISS

Lips fit like jigsaw pieces from different designs finding their perfect place in this chaotic collage of existence.

Webbed into each other's skins all they know now is the taste of those aphrodisiac doses they kept sipping and the rosy red ripples they created right after.

Stagnation
OF THOUGHTS

WEIGH IT

The weight of
my love
crushing you.

But,

the weight of
your head
is what my
shoulder asks
for.

THE EVERY

Every thought been thought,
Every song already sung,
Every term of endearment used,
Is there any room left for one to innovate;
       The mind itself losing track of thoughts.

Every action been reacted to,
Every flight already flown,
Every piece of clothing worn,
Is there any new face out there;
       The mask itself losing its act.

Every poem been recited,
Every touch already touched,
Every apple of the eye seen,
Is there any creation left sacred anymore;
       The pen itself losing its ink.

Every love been loved,
Every dream already dreamt,
Every ward of habit broken,
Is there any human humane;
       The word itself losing its meaning.

PRESERVATION

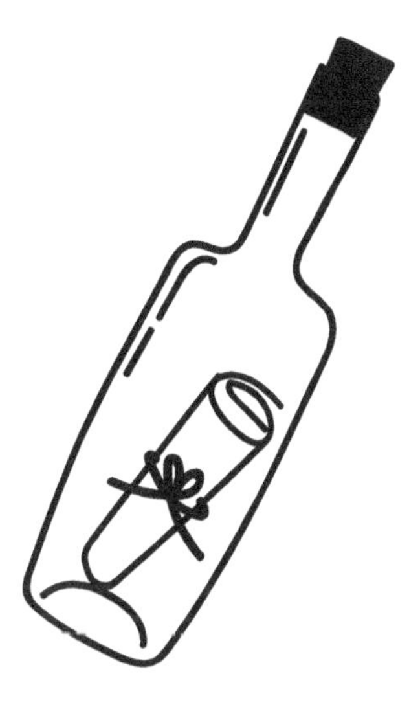

Some things I
keep pondering
on but never find
an answer to and I
still keep getting
washed off to the
shores just to be
found by someone
who preserves me
for a while longer.

CLOSEST

That's the closest you'd get,
To being just more than just a coincidence.

That's the closest I'd get,
To blossoming into the image you need.

That's the closest you'd get,
To pricking me with the needles you poke.

That's the closest I'd get,
To making sure you're okay.

That's the closest you'd get,
To changing the nuts and bolts of me.

That's the closest I'd get,
To fitting into the framework you've made.

That's the closest you'd get,
To loving me,

And that's the closest I'd get,
To being rather hated.

NOT A SHOULDER

I don't want to write for you,
I don't want to feel for you,
I don't want to love you,
Not anymore.

I don't see me in us,
I don't see you in us,
I don't see love in us,
Not anymore.

I don't know why,
I don't know when,
I don't where,
Will we find each other again.

Stuck in these don'ts,
I lie to myself, of what I've become,
I lie to myself, of what we've become,
I lean on a shoulder that's barely there.

DNA LOVE

Fates twisted in spirals,
Of the two strands,
Of dreams and DNAs,
Love lost..

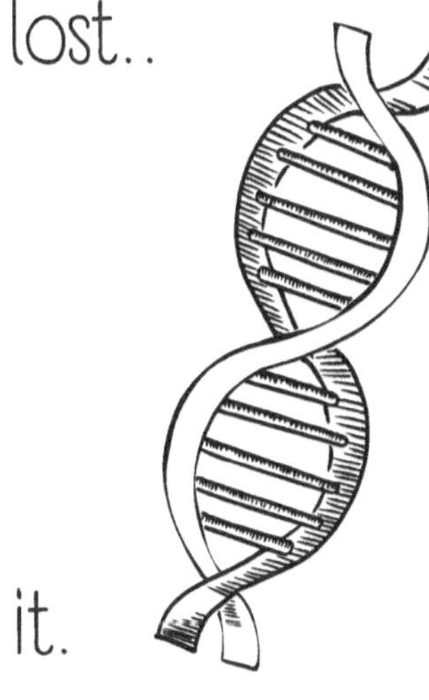

in it.

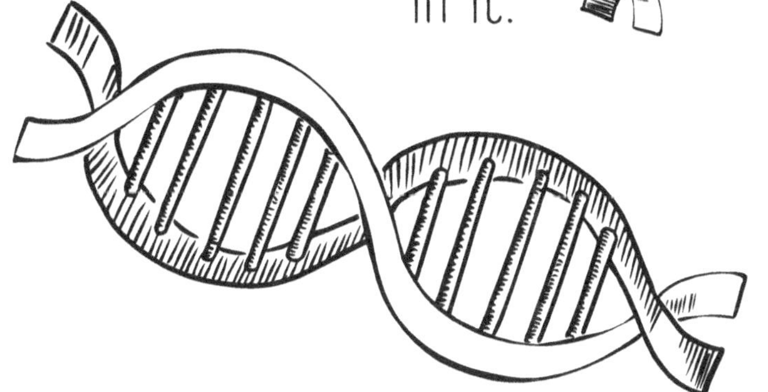

Kid I am, numb I don't wanna be.
Looking at dots connect,
Looking at emotions making sense,
Looking at everything fitting in its own space.

Feeling empty, a vast ocean turning into vapours,
In seconds life takes a turn,
I feel and I am a rock again,
Hard and motionless again.

Innocent I was, grown up I try to be,
Innocence I miss, is it that you try to find,
Try finding, help me find it too,
Have lost it a while back, lost myself with it too.

Popping of bubbles on the surface,
On the sea bed of feelings I wonder,
As shallow as the beach, oh NO,
As deep as an ocean I am.

FEEL IT FOR ME

Try understanding me, knowing me,
Tired of the job I am,
Give me the pleasure of speaking without speaking,
Jaws are hurting now.

Having dinner at breakfast time,
Have eaten my self up,
So hungry to feel something,
This fast isn't really working out for me.

Kill me now, or bring me back to life,
Make me feel, or crush me like a bottle,
Hanging is something which is a bit tough,
Cut me out. Give me wings. Let me fly.

A TIDE

A roof with holes,
In a room full of souls,
Dripping their intellect,
To see what they can collect.

A storm without intent,
In a heart that's never content,
Tripping away in a void,
Not to be toyed.

A being with many faults,
Locked away in vaults,
Tipping over to the dark side,
To rise and fall like a tide.

AM I ME?

For some time now I think, I'm not me.
I was not me,
When they say I lied.
I was not me,
When I say, I had died.

It was me though,
When I apologized,
It was me though,
When I cried.

I was not me then,
When I cheated,
I was not me when,
I was toxic.

It was my pain talking,
It was my hurt expressing,
It was my insecurity very secure,
It was just the image I needed,
Didn't want it though.

Maybe I'm emotional,
Maybe I'm naive,
Maybe I'm trustworthy,
Maybe I'm just in the moment,
Maybe I'm more about the flux,
Maybe I'm more about the flow,
Maybe I'm more of me,
Much much more of me,
Which is why you don't see it,
That far along the horizon,
Clouded by your own judgments,
The boundary shimmers,
Like an oasis in a dry desert.

Walking on this path,
From I to me,
Is a dangerous one because,
Neither me nor the ones around,
Know the difference.

Sometimes I wonder, how would it have been
if 'I' didn't exist in the first place,
Would you say, That is still me?

PATTERN

The moulding of repeating patterns,
Of shapes and of distorted beings,
Drunk on emotions and
infused potions,
Of poisons and elixirs,
I...

S

A

N

K.

LET'S GO BACK THERE

There was a time,
When we would just sway,
Around each other's thoughts,
Around each other's lives;
Let's go back there.

There was a space,
Where neither of us hurt,
Nor would we stay hurt for,
Any longer than it takes to say "hello";
Let's go back there.

There were many rhymes,
Creating dynamic symphonies,
Filling up with not just joy,
But a relief of the pain which is no longer there;
Let's go back there.

There was a time,
When we were just friends,
Romanticizing about romance,
But no more, we're in love now;

Let's find out what lies ahead,
Do you still want to fly with me?

THE STREET

Lonely I walk, thinking I'm a fool,
Fooling myself with words,
Words which I tell myself,
Selflessly selling my soul.

Keeping up with the age of my body,
Catching up to the social norms,
I wait, I sit, I cry, I weep,
One notices, other does not.

Walking back on my tracks,
Tracks covered with regret,
Regret is what I fear not,
Fear is what I truly fear.

DON'T LET GO JUST YET

Take me into the spirals and sing me lullabies,
Make me feel like the tornado causing devastation,
For the sake of saving though,
Try capturing as much of me, don't let me go just yet.

Fickle-minded I am, steadiness not my forte,
I'm now walking on the sharp side of the knife,
You so gently plunge into my existence,
Bleeding I am, don't pull it out yet.

Sorrow, shame, regret, lust, turning me into dust,
Collect me into the pot of your desires,
Cover it with the red shroud of selves that came before,
Skin so soft, don't flow it in the river yet.

Subjects of time we are in the kingdom of surreal worlds,
What's unreal becomes our reality,
What's unusual becomes our mystery,
For you to keep, don't you please let it go just yet.

Crashing
UNTO THE SHORE

UNTOUCH YOU

Go into your box,
Of the kind of Love,
I want from you,
And you too;
Making a whole,
Out of bits and pieces,
Out of the gestures,
Done and undone.

Go through my being,
Of different boxes,
You've put me in,
Interesting enough a read?
Or is it a mirror,
Of how you see,
Through all the layers,
The sheets that separate us.

Go away now,
A lil farther away,
I'm burning,
The Phoenix, not me;
The farther you go,
The lesser you see,
The deeper I get,
The ashes you see, thats me.

Come close,
Close enough to give goosebumps,
Not that close, no,
Proximity causing the split;
Parting me,
One by one,
Slices of a being,
Served and ready to be eaten.

Touch me,
My soul,
Caress it,
Give it the boxed love;
I'll make it whole,
I'll make it interesting,
I'll set the distance,
And I'll cause the split.

PRESERVATION (PT. 2)

Some things we keep pondering on but never find an answer to and I still rush to the shores just to crash into the rocks, just to preserve more questions to which there are no answers.

FLY BACK DOWN

Let's forget we ever,
Expressed what we felt,
Ever remembered what we had,
Memorized, to the last bit.

Doesn't it feel nice,
And warm and fuzzy?
Every experience is a new one,
Every emotion is the first you've ever felt.

Let's now come back to reality,
Where it haunts our existence,
But reminds us the pinnacle,
We last reached.

The peak only reaches new heights,
Self gets more expressive,
More vulnerable to the vibes,
To the dots we connect.

We hustle our way in,
Dive into it from the sky,
Trek up to the snowy peaks,
Just to fly back down.

STATES

State of the world,
State of the mind,
State of the body,
State of emotions;

None matter, when it all comes

t
u
m
b
l
i
n
g
d
o
w
n.

MOMENT

He swings by and a splash of perfume hits me;
He flashes his teeth in the most sheepish manner possible,
"Are you mad at me?", he asks,
Faking the best expression I say, "No".

He moves me, shakes the very foundation,
Controls my every move without any controls,
Forgets me when I'm lost,
And kisses me when I'm around.

At his dispense, I hang always,
Expectations hundreds I carry, fulfilled are none,
Crazy he gets me with his presence,
I wish I could have had his attention for a while longer.

He lies in my bed, me on him,
Or his head resting on my bare chest,
The touch itself causing ecstasy,
For a moment it lasts,
And passes away.

BLINK

He says bye, and I blink,
Blink again to see what
he really meant,
Finding meaning in
meaningless words,
Words to push me away.

THE KILL

A sorrow so deep,
One cannot even rely,
On his own memory,
Of what he sowed once,
He saw it reap.

Rhymes and realms,
Territories and tales,
A sermon's futility,
A vermin's tentacle,
Is all he had to hold.

A knife that was drawn,
A poison that didn't work,
A jump that was never flown,
A life worth dying for,
Why not die, the child ponders.

Complex truths perplex him,
Tease by tease,
Simple beings cripple him,
Piece by piece,
Secretly losing himself in Harlem.

Art evades him,
Just as humans do,
And he evades art,
Just as a deer pounces,
While the lioness roars for the kill;

Does he live?

We shall never know the lore.

ENOUGH

Never enough
is it to just
stay calm,
Not enough
to sit by the
palm,

Enough if it
had been,
Enough love
wouldn't have
been left
behind.

I DID

Let's phrase metaphors into sentences,
They no longer suffice as alternatives,
Every word is spoken clearly, the emotion,
Expressed and accounted for.

Let's make poetry lose its mystery,
Why keep things from the reader,
Open for interpretation, open for exploitation,
A sentenced life for the poem.

Let's build walls up, real ones this time,
Crumbling them gets one in a soup,
Destination or not, the climb or not,
Roused egos higher than the walls.

Let's love one another across these veils,
Of iridescent imaginary imagery,
In the utopia, in the fantasy world,
Survived none.

The bard, the lover, the paradise, the halo,
Oh, back in the vicious cycle I find myself,
Myself trying to get out of the swamp,
 did.

POINTLESS

Thoughts profuse,
Calling a truce,
Don't quiet down,
As if that would magically happen,

This is pointless.
I'm just blah.

TOXIC

My souls
infused in
the poison
that life
gives,

Just
breathing
everyday
becomes a
detox from
the toxic
me.

SINNER I AM

Sin is mine, sinner I am,
Mistakes are mine, mistaken I'm not,
Yes, entitled you are to hurt me,
But would you really?

Taken for granted I am always,
Was better off being a stone,
Steal this stone from everyone,
Don't steal yourself from me.

1 percent I do, making up to 100 is your job,
Religiously the job is done,
Wrongs I do, rights I do,
Wrongs matter, rights do not.

DROWNING AGAIN

Being in love should feel like butterflies and sunflowers,
but it hurts to keep being in love.
Why does it become this spiral that I can never escape?

Shouldn't love feel like flying,
Instead, it feels like free-falling, you're flying for a while
but then the weightlessness becomes a fear of dying
in the next two seconds.

The end comes nearer, do you have a parachute though?

The seconds become eternities you would've otherwise lived,
Does the parachute work though?

The lives you led become a life that would be no more,
Are you sure you're not diving into some deep ocean, again?
Drowning again?

SEDUCING (PT. 2)

A fog that has settled on the flowing rivers never
Stopped getting more translucent.
For me to see, for him to be,
It never did seem that difficult.

But it was and it is what it never seemed to be,
A bouquet of thorns and roses.

Bleeding out,
The fingers finished,
What his lips started;

A little rebellion, A little joy.

LAST THINGS, LAST TIME

Last things were said,
Last time the void was filled,
The knife pulled out,
Leaving a bloody trail behind.

Last things were seen,
Last time the stare made,
The red shroud of ashes flew,
Into the river of time.

Last things were smelt,
Last time the aroma infused,
The breath that left the lungs,
Gushed out like hurricanes on an empty island.

Last things were heard,
Last time the talk happened,
Echoing like thunder in a sandstorm,
Sounding far deeper than farther.

Last things were felt,
Last time the emotional out,
The mystery solved now,
By the surrealistic realist,
I am finally me now.

Taking Back
WHAT I LEARNT

PHASES

New phase, new page,
I write, I flirt,
With the pen, with the ink,
The impressions of the torn paper I threw,
Still engraved deeper than it looks on the new page.

Beginning this is, or end it seems,
Sun rising in the east,
But finding the disappearing moon more beautiful,
White light it sheds on the sheets I write,
Colors I look for in the clouded thoughts I put out.

Cool calm breeze I feel,
Chirpy birds await,
Finding the silence more disturbing,
Touch of my feet to the cold-marble floor,
I wonder,
Sand is not the only place one loses their existence.

SELFISH ME

The heart pounds even more than it usually does,
Thoughts gushing out of the head,
The mind does not really bring the heart back to sanity,
Answering those questions to which there are no answers.

The leg twitches as if it has to run somewhere right now,
Second thoughts shout out, "Stay, stay put, right there!",
You hold your ground, get crushed to bits and pieces,
And then you recreate, regenerate into something,
That makes you, YOU.

The initial butterflies in the tummy,
turn into worms eating you up from the inside,
You get empty, empty like one clears out
The apartment of the emotions you once shared,
The slate being clean now is washed,
To the last dust of chalk that remains,
Paint it with new colours,
At least with your own colour,
Loving yourself,
Being Selfish.

Crickets and Ballads

He can't bear the thought,
I can't either.
A cure, a lure,
A regret, a debt;
That I've been paying,
My dues of what life,
I know naught of.

He can't but feel,
I can't either.
A lore, a gore,
A cry, a try;
That keeps me from choosing,
Death over living,
Others over 'me'.

He can never let go,
I never could either.
A study, a story,
A sting, a ring;
That saved me for a latter day,
Endless metaphors a poem,
It's him that it's from.

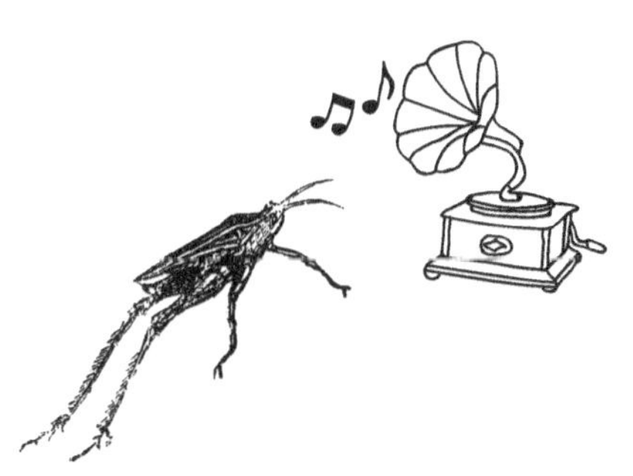

He can love though,
I can as well.
A bond, a fond,
A ballad, another ballad;
That's sung by his crickets,
And his smile and mine,
It's nuances and us.
Ah, the beautiful US.

THE STREET (PT.2)

A hand held mine, thinking I'm lonely,
Lonely I was surrounded by people,
People who lusted me,
Me who loved them back.

Keeping up with what I have accomplished,
All caught up with the social norms,
I giggle, I meddle, I laugh, I smile,
A hand notices, and holds mine tight.

Walking forward on the path not taken,
Taken by the sunshine glare,
Glare if you must, but love,
Love is what I truly love now.

CATHARSIS (IMPENDING)

They walk in a chasm,
Unknowing of the shadows,
Acknowledging them,
Alluring them,
To fall;
Let's fly though.

They stroll strategically,
Growing on each other,
A symbiotic being lost,
In translation,
To be found;
Let's not pry though.

They dive together,
In unchartered territories,
Charring memories,
Creating the chaos,
To resolve;
Let's allow the catharsis to happen now.

A BOON OR A BANE

Some experiences build you,
Some break you,
Some keep you hanging,
Trishanku is the being I am.

Few losses have been mourned,
Few gains have been celebrated,
Fewer moments have life in them,
Accountant is the being I am.

Many times the game has been played,
Many times the game has played me,
Many more times the play has been interesting,
Gambler is the being I am.

Much has been interpreted,
Much has been made known,
Much more has been created too,
Artist is the being I am.

Little has been the reality,
Little has been a fantasy,
Even more little the actual being,
Child is the being I was.

AN AFTERTHOUGHT

Just as an afterthought I doubt I want attention anymore.

I think I.. I.. I..
I simply miss the simplicity.
I truly miss the truth.
I sadly miss the sadness.
I humbly miss the humility.

That line you'd cross over to keep me from writing, just feeling it right
then and releasing its grip on me.

That line you'd walk on to balance the two worlds that are now either a
zero or a one.

I wish I could just not feel anymore towards anything or anyone;
Just so that I could maybe feel a little numb,
Before the last needle is pricked.
Just so that I could maybe stop being so paradoxical, feeling 'numbness'.

The afterthought remains an afterthought,
Never to be expressed but felt,
With every inch of the skin as it dances to the waves,
To the shivers,
To the Lover's voice,
His kiss, his embrace,
Lost in the thought,
And then the afterthought.

Self-Care

Touch yourself. Touch your body. Maybe it'll be more caressing than how carelessly people touch.

Touch your heart. Feel it beat. Maybe it has bearing against your chest all this while to make you realize it's beating just for you.

Touch your mind. Hear it speak. Maybe it has been thinking of you and wondering why these thoughts come to it, as clueless as you are.

You're not alone.

हम थे, अब कौन है?

मैं जो हूँ आज, उसका कोई इल्म नहीं है,

जो मैं कल था, उसका कोई ज़िक्र नहीं है,

ज़िक्र तो उनका हो, जिनसे कोई तालुख है,

जो मैं कल था, उसका और मेरा तालुख हि

क्या है?

Calming Vastness

IN THE WORLD AFTER

RESSURECTION

I died some time ago.

Resurrected I was by a soul so
pure that just being around,
one pays penance for the sins
committed.

The blurry background is all
clear to me now.
Concentrating on self,
The cuts and buts,
Bruises and piercings,
Pain of the past,
Drain of the future
That will soon be here.

Being in the present would
truly be a gift now.

LABELLED LOVE

They say love surpasses all labels,
and we keep labelling love for
ourselves; just so that the love
makes a little more sense to us.

Love is so many things that
language just
cannot articulate.

Love is more than me or you. It is
for us to believe that there are
certain things that one might never
be able to explain,
only experience.

WOULD I?

Stone cold I feel,
Paradoxes they seal,
If I would ever heal,
Would I still be this still?

A time spent in abyss,
Maybe something was amiss,
If I would ever miss,
Would I piece my peace?

Trying too hard to write,
Letting the wrongs become right,
If I would ever have that sight,
Would I plate my plight?

A quiet that settles,
On frozen petals,
If I would ever rhyme,
Would I time it this time?

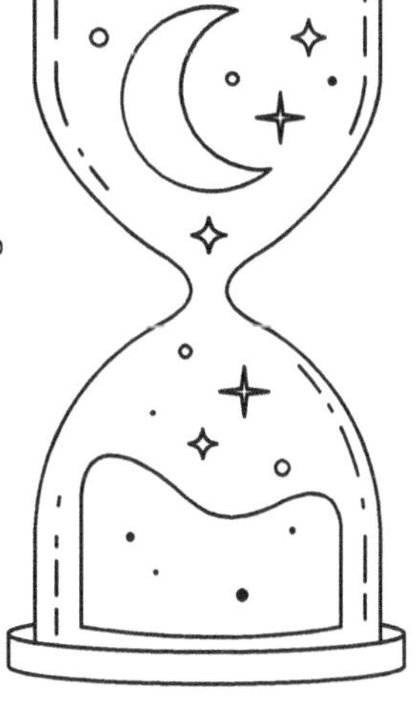

BE IN MY SHOES

How do I make you understand?
How would you know?
How do you make me understand?
How would I know?

Right, you don't get it,
You don't have to;
Yes, I don't get it either,
I don't have to.

Feel this for me,
Take away the pain,
Be there for me,
Doesn't matter if you're in pain.

The chords we strike,
The notes we sing,
The instruments we play,
The symphonies we make.

Is it worth the effort?
Is it worth the time?
Is it worth the emotions?
Be in my shoes and see.

IT IS.

इस ज़िंदगी में

इस ज़िंदगी में जीना सीख लीजिये,

हमें भुला के कोई आलाप हि गा लीजिये,

हम तो रहे दीवाने आपकी मुस्कुराहट के,

शब्द नहीं रहंगे, ये ग़ालिब भी न रहेंगा,

रहेगा ये प्यार.. इसे ना भूला दीजिए।

Epilogue

As I look back at the things this teenage self of mine wrote in this book years ago, I am drawn to discovering the stories that unfolded after the calming vastness. These stories taught me that the change in seasons is much like the shifts in our own lives, its storms, and ours. Over time, the very nature of love has transformed for me, shaping how I show and share it.

Each moment I've lived through has left a meaningful mark on my life's journey. With this in mind, I remain open to new experiences, growing and evolving with all kinds of relationships around me. My journey is about being, and adapting to the changes that come while I flow with the currents of the ocean.

Never thought there would be another stage,
Past all that calming vastness,
The very feeling engulfs me,
Submerged, subversive, submissive,
And me looking for a submarine,
To save me from drowning,
To save me from my own ocean,
To save me from the moon,
To save me from the lagoon.

Never thought there would be another emotion,
That I haven't yet experienced,
On the roller coaster of life,
Twisted twilights, intertwined,
With a version of my own self,
To live a life of lie,
To live my own truth,
To live the life of loss,
To live just to die yet again.

Never thought there would be another moment,
Just as special as the last one,
These peaks are what I'm scared of,
Unreachable, undesirable urns,
Of ashes I collected in that moment,
To see what I needed to,
To see that what is hidden,
To see myself in a new light,
To see my soulmate and yet lose my soul.

NEVER THOUGHT

Other books by Vrujen

www.ingramcontent.com/pod-product-compliance
Lightning Source LLC
Chambersburg PA
CBHW021408150726
47989CB00005B/2454